Capitalism, Morality and Markets

Capitalism, Morality and Markets

BRIAN GRIFFITHS
ROBERT A. SIRICO
NORMAN BARRY
FRANK FIELD

The Institute of Economic Affairs

First published in Great Britain in 2001 by
The Institute of Economic Affairs
2 Lord North Street
Westminster
London sw1p 3lb
in association with Profile Books Ltd

A CIP catalogue record for this book is available from the British Library.

isbn 0 255 36496 2

Many IEA publications are translated into languages other than English or are
reprinted. Permission to translate or to reprint should be sought from the
General Director at the address above.

Typeset in Stone by MacGuru
info@macguru.org.uk

Printed and bound in Great Britain by Hobbs the Printers

CONTENTS

THE AUTHORS

Lord Griffiths of Fforestfach

Brian Griffiths taught at the London School of Economics from 1965 to 1976, and was appointed Professor of Banking and International Finance at City University in 1976. He was Dean of the City University Business School from 1982 to 1985 and a director of the Bank of England from 1983 to 1985.

He served as head of the Prime Minister's Policy Unit from 1985 until 1990. In his role as special advisor to Margaret Thatcher he was responsible for domestic policy-making and was one of the chief architects of the government's privatisation and deregulation programmes. On leaving No. 10 he was made a member of the House of Lords.

Since then, Lord Griffiths has been Vice Chairman of Goldman Sachs (Europe) and an international advisor to Goldman Sachs concerned with strategic issues relating to their UK and Asian operations, business development activities worldwide and principal investments. He is chairman of two companies, Trillium and Westminster Health Care, and a non-executive director of Times Newspaper Holdings Ltd, Herman Miller Inc., ServiceMaster and the English, Welsh and Scottish Railway.

From 1991 to 2000 he was Chairman of the Centre for Policy Studies, the think tank set up by Keith Joseph and Margaret

Thatcher, where he is still a member of the board. He is also Chairman of the Archbishop of Canterbury's Lambeth Trust and Christian Responsibility in Public Affairs.

Father Robert A. Sirico

Revd Robert A. Sirico received his Master of Divinity degree from the Catholic University of America following undergraduate study at the University of Southern California and the University of London. In 1990, he co-founded the Acton Institute with Kris Alan Mauren. As President of the Acton Institute, Fr Sirico lectures at colleges, universities, and business organisations throughout the US and abroad. His writings on religious, political, economic and social matters have been published in a variety of journals.

In April 1999, Fr Sirico was awarded an honorary doctorate in Christian Ethics from the Franciscan University of Steubenville. He is a member of the Mont Pèlerin Society, the American Academy of Religion, the Philadelphia Society and the Board of Advisors of the Civic Institute in Prague. He also served on the Michigan Civil Rights Commission from 1994 to 1998.

Fr Sirico's pastoral ministry has included a chaplaincy to Aids patients at the National Institute of Health and the recent founding of a new community, St Philip Neri House in Kalamazoo, Michigan.

Professor Norman Barry

Norman Barry is Professor of Social and Political Theory at the University of Buckingham. His research interests include analytical political philosophy, welfare theory and business ethics. His books include *Hayek's Social and Economic Philosophy*; *On Classical Liberalism and Libertarianism*; *The New Right*; *Welfare and Business Ethics*. He has been Visiting Scholar at the Social Philosophy and Policy Center, Bowling Green State University, Ohio and Liberty Fund, Indianapolis. He is a member of the Academic Advisory Councils of the Institute of Economic Affairs and the David Hume Institute (Edinburgh).

Rt Hon. Frank Field MP

Frank Field was Director of the Child Poverty Action Group from 1969 to 1979 and Director of the Low Pay Unit from 1974 to 1980. He was elected Member of Parliament for Birkenhead in 1979.

He is a former front bench spokesman on education and social security and former Chairman of the Social Security Select Committee. He was Minister for Welfare Reform, Department of Social Security from 1997 to 1998. He has an honorary doctorate of law from the University of Warwick and an honorary doctorate of science from Southampton University.

11-13

BK Title!

FOREWORD

NIP

*Colin
Robinson*

'Morality and markets' has been a recurring theme of Institute publications over the years. In recent times, the Hayek Memorial Lectures in 1993 and 1998, by Professors Michael Novak and Jonathan Sacks respectively, were both on that subject.[1] There are many issues which can be addressed as part of this general theme – for example, whether moral and ethical values are independent or whether they evolve through market processes, and whether or not companies should have moral standards.

To allow continued discussion of these many issues, the Institute began in June and July 2000 a series of lectures which will take place annually, entitled 'The Templeton Forum on Markets and Morality'. The idea for the series, and the original endowment which made it possible, came from Michael Novak who won the Templeton Prize for Progress in Religion in 1994 and credited the Institute of Economic Affairs with part of the responsibility for this recognition of his work. His endowment was generously matched by the John Templeton Foundation.

In the first series, we were fortunate to hear four outstanding papers, each covering quite different ground. Lord Griffiths of Fforestfach gave the first lecture, under the chairmanship of Sir

---

1   Michael Novak, 'Two Moral Ideals for Business', *Economic Affairs*, September–October 1993; and Jonathan Sacks, *Morals and Markets*, IEA Occasional Paper 108, 1999.

Stanley Kalms. The second was by Father Robert Sirico, chaired by Revd David Prior. Professor Norman Barry's third lecture was chaired by Revd Dr Hugh Rayment-Pickard. The final lecture, by Rt Hon. Frank Field MP, was chaired by Clive Wright. Revised versions of the four lectures are reprinted in this volume.

Lord Griffiths considers the business corporation as a moral community. He points out that research into the performance of corporations has shown that the existence of shared values is an important element in their success. He goes on to discuss whether or not corporations can function without moral standards, concluding that 'an independent moral standard is not only something which is good in itself but is also in the interests of shareholders and employees'. In his view, the corporation has become 'an important standard bearer of values in society'.

The subject chosen by Father Robert Sirico of the Acton Institute was 'The Culture of Virtue, the Culture of the Market'. His point of departure is the commonly expressed view that markets turn a person into '*Homo economicus*', valued only for his or her productive potential. Father Sirico agrees that the 'profit and loss system is not the sum total of human community', but he argues that the accomplishments of business directly help advance social prosperity, health and human welfare. So the market is a necessary ally for a 'social order which respects human dignity'.

Professor Norman Barry analyses the claim that capitalism is 'ethically deficient' and finds it wanting. He argues that the market system is 'morally self-sufficient and . . . develops its own codes of conduct'. Business morality 'develops spontaneously through the development of those constraints on immediate gratification which the market system undoubtedly requires'. He criticises 'stakeholder' theories of business ethics and contends that ethical conduct by business simply requires companies to follow rules and conventions which make for long-run success.

The final paper, by Rt Hon. Frank Field MP, addresses a specific subject on which he is an acknowledged expert – markets and the provision of a minimum income in retirement. Mr Field says that, though he is 'a fully paid-up member of the market brigade', there are some areas in which markets cannot achieve socially desirable goals. Provision of a 'decent minimum income in retirement' is one of those. Some compulsion is required, as in his own 'New Stakeholder Proposal', prepared when he was a government minister, which is 'the only workable scheme to break the link between retirement and poverty'.

As always in Institute publications, this varied collection of papers – designed to stimulate thought about the relationship between moral values and markets – represents the views of the authors, not those of the Institute (which has no corporate view), its managing trustees, Academic Advisory Council members or senior staff. Other aspects of the morality and markets debate will be explored in the Templeton Forum in 2001.

COLIN ROBINSON
Editorial Director, Institute of Economic Affairs
Professor of Economics, University of Surrey
January 2001

Capitalism, Morality and Markets

1   THE BUSINESS CORPORATION AS A MORAL COMMUNITY[1]
Lord Griffiths of Fforestfach

The significance of 'values' in explaining the performance of business corporations is a relatively recent emphasis in management thinking. The subject came to prominence in the US in the 1970s, after a decade in which US business had seen its fortunes wane because of the inroads made by Japanese automobile and electronics companies into the American market. This prompted a good deal of soul searching by the American business community, which in turn led to extensive research analysing the comparative performance of US corporations.

The conclusion of this work was that one significant factor in explaining the superior performance of certain corporations was the shared values of the corporation itself: namely that set of beliefs and values which were championed throughout the organisation and which formed the basis of its corporate culture. Subsequent research conducted at the Harvard Business School confirmed the significance of shared values in influencing corporate performance, which was one factor which led to a major shift in management thinking in the 1980s with less emphasis placed on management science, corporate planning and economies of scale and much greater focus on the customer, the contribution of the

---

1   This chapter draws heavily on the Hansen-Wessner lecture given at the Said Business School, University of Oxford, October 1999, which was sponsored by the ServiceMaster Foundation.

individual employee and the importance of corporate culture. Since then the subject of values has remained a key item on the agenda of US corporations and increasingly of business corporations in other countries as well.

As part of this ongoing debate about the significance of values in business, I wish to examine five questions. What is a moral standard in business? Can a corporation function without a moral standard? From where can the business corporation derive a moral standard? How does the corporation function and implement a moral standard in a pluralistic society? And how significant is the corporation because it is a bearer of a moral standard? These are questions which I believe are and certainly should be of concern to the management of all public companies.

What is a moral standard in business?

It is a set of values, norms or ethical principles which are accepted as a benchmark, reference point or criterion for all who work within the company and which as a consequence will guide and influence behaviour. By this is meant not just that certain kinds of behaviour are deemed acceptable or unacceptable, but something stronger: namely that these kinds of behaviour are also categorised as good or bad, right or wrong. This moral standard will be the genesis of the ethical demands made upon each employee and the raw material from which the corporation creates its distinctive ethos and culture. Such a standard is set out in the business principles or mission statements of the corporation and reinforced by statements from the chairman, the chief executive officer and others in positions of leadership. It is the binding principle which enables the corporation to act as a corpus, unified in attitude and practice. It is because of the emphasis corporations now place on establishing values and maintaining ethical standards that modern corporations can and should be conceived of as moral communities.

The question of what should be included in a company's moral standard and the way in which it is expressed will vary from company to company. But in examining the statements of a variety of companies there are recurring themes: the need for integrity, transparency, honesty and telling the truth; a respect for the individual person because of his or her innate dignity as a fellow human being; a sense of fairness in the way people are treated; the ideal of service, especially in relation to customers but also in the style of leadership shown by executives; the value of teamwork; the responsibility of the corporation to respect the environment; and a commitment to support those communities in which the corporation has facilities. In fact, these themes appear so frequently in different sectors, different countries, different continents and different cultures, that they become less a collection of disparate values chosen by individual companies and more and more a set of universals.

Every creed, sooner or later, will ask its adherents to 'pick up the tab' and a moral standard in business is no exception. A moral standard makes strenuous demands, taking the corporation beyond the boundary of the legal requirement. It may require a corporation to refuse a piece of business, to invest heavily in developing its people, or to sort out problems without resort to lawyers, all of which will adversely affect short-term profitability but which at the same time demonstrate its commitment to the standard. For when a chairman or chief executive stands up to declare that his corporation operates a moral standard, he is saying that it not only makes a difference to the way his corporation does business but that it actually determines that way.

Can a corporation function without a moral standard?

In principle, the answer to this question must be yes: a corporation could operate with a moral standard, an amoral standard or an immoral standard. A corporation which carried on its activities according to an immoral standard, however, would quickly find itself in conflict with the law and with government. One example of such a business might be organised crime, another a corporation which set out to evade (not avoid) the tax authorities, another a corporation which knowingly traded in services or products classified as prohibited, such as certain kinds of drugs dealings, the sale of human embryos and the sale and purchase of children. These corporations would not only trade in products which would be described as immoral: they would also engage in activities which would inevitably result in extortion, violence and fraud. Executives discovered running such corporations would face financial penalties, criminal prosecution and possible imprisonment.

A company which operated with an immoral standard could function in the short term but it is difficult to see how it could possibly be viable in the longer term.

A more intriguing question is whether a corporation can function on an amoral standard. The single objective of such a corporation would be the maximisation of profit. The corporation would operate within the law, but would be unconcerned with moral principles. It would question whether a policy or action was legal or illegal but not whether it was right or wrong. Morality would be outside the scope of business. Its standard of honesty would be rooted in expediency, personal integrity would be unimportant and individuals valued only in proportion to their contribution to the bottom line.

A company with an amoral standard would be a cold, bleak and insecure environment in which to work. Loyalty would not exist. A person's commitment to honour a promise would forever remain in doubt. There would be no trust. The drawing up of contracts would be lengthy, tiresome and complex. Negotiating executive compensation plans would become a headache. Setting up a joint venture would be a nightmare because one could never be sure if the other side was telling the truth. The internal audit function would need strengthening. Due diligence would become a long and tedious affair and a significant obstacle to acquisitions. There would be a constant stream of disputes, conflict and litigation. The commitment made by members of the executive team to the future of the company would be uncertain. One would never know whether a colleague had declared his or her true interests in matters affecting the business. Because of its reputation recruitment of staff would be difficult. One major consequence of an amoral culture is that the cost of doing business, what economists term 'transactions cost', would be that much greater, so that the firm would soon find itself at a competitive disadvantage.

Perhaps the person who most successfully portrayed the characteristics of an amoral economy was Bernard Mandeville in *The Fable of the Bees: or Private Vices, Publick Benefits*, which was first published in 1714 and based on a poem published nine years earlier, 'The Grumbling Hive or Knaves turned Honest'.[2] In describing the

---

2   Bernard Mandeville, *The Fable of the Bees: or Private Vices, Publick Benefits*, Oxford, Clarendon Press, 1924. Republished Liberty Press, Indianapolis 1988.

flourishing beehive as a metaphor for a successful commercial trading nation such as the England of his day, Mandeville singled out dishonesty, selfishness and devotion to vice as the emotions which lay at the root of prosperity. Merchants, soldiers, lawyers, doctors, judges, statesmen – all were implicated,

> Millions endeavouring to supply
> each other's lust and vanity

Distinguishing commerce from virtue ('Religion is one thing and Trade is another') he argued that a permissive attitude to the vices and selfishness of the bees would lead to an extension of the division of labour, a widening of the market and a consequent growth in trade which would be to everyone's benefit. His observation of the hive therefore was:

> Thus every part was full of vice
> Yet the whole mass an earthly paradise

Problems only arose when through a public display of blatant hypocrisy the Knaves prayed to the gods for honesty, a prayer which Jove allowed to be answered, with disastrous results. Pride and luxury gradually decreased, there was less trade, arts and crafts were neglected and through the decline of their vices the bees discovered that they lost all their greatness. The concluding moral is that:

> Fools only strive
> To make a Great and Honest Hive,
> T'enjoy the World's Conveniencies
> Be fam'd in War, yet live in Ease,
> Without great Vices is a vain
> Eutopia seated in the Brain

The vain utopia he had in mind was the practice of a Christian ethic of self-restraint and charity, which alas by removing the vices would simply lead to the impoverishment of the nation. Not surprisingly the publication of the fable created a great stir and was presented before the Grand Jury of Middlesex as a public nuisance. Even Adam Smith, who might be considered the founder of modern capitalism, was in his *Theory of Moral Sentiments*[3] decidedly critical of Mandeville because of his sophistry in identifying virtue with complete self-denial and his moral nihilism in refusing to lay out any criterion which would distinguish moral good from evil.

Perhaps the most characteristic feature of the amoral approach today is the cry that business should be concerned with the maximisation of profit and nothing else. Management is elected by shareholders, so the argument goes, to look after their interests and should steer clear of acting as trustees for any other. The business of business is business in which a moral standard has no relevance. However not even Milton Friedman in his well-known essay 'The Social Responsibility of Business is to Increase its Profits'[4] suggests that the sole objective of business should be to maximise profits: what he says is that business executives should 'conduct business in accordance with their desires, which generally will be to make as much money as possible while conforming to the basic rules of society', but then, and this is very important, he qualifies the 'basic rules of society' to include 'both those embodied in law and those embodied in ethical custom', so making it clear that the

---

3   Adam Smith, *The Theory of Moral Sentiments*, 1759, pp. 485–6.

4   Milton Friedman, 'The Social Responsibility of Business is to Increase Its Profits'. Reprinted in *Ethical Theory and Business*, T. Beauchamp and N. Bowie (eds.), Englewood Cliffs, New Jersey, Prentice Hall, 1988.

pursuit of profit need not be inconsistent with respect for cultural norms or a moral standard.

The third alternative is a corporation which operates with a moral standard. The leadership of the corporation would set out its distinct values which would typically include honesty, reliability and service: a regard for the importance of the individual and his or her personal development; the ability to be part of a team and put the interests of the team before one's own; and responsibility to others, both within and outside the organisation. The reasons the leadership of a corporation may decide to have an explicit moral standard may be many and complex, but if executives and employees are convinced of their intrinsic worth, one of the consequences of this approach will be to create a high degree of trust within the organisation.

Within a company in which people trust each other a strong team spirit will develop. Internal rules and regulations will need to be spelt out in less detail. The compliance, internal audit and supervisory functions will not need to be so extensive. The statements of leaders will be accepted at face value. Such companies will be named as preferred employers, so making the recruitment of good quality staff much easier. Between such companies there will be less need for lengthy and complex contracts. All of these are benefits which result from trust; and trust is an example of what an economist would term 'externalities'. They are goods which have tangible economic value and which increase the productivity of a company's operation, but they are not commodities which can be bought and sold on the open market.

A corporation with an effective moral standard therefore will not only have lower transactions costs but will develop over time a strong culture based on trust, so that the adoption of a moral standard will become a source of competitive advantage.

The answer to the first question therefore, 'Can a corporation function without a moral standard?', is in principle yes, but in practice extremely unlikely, especially if it wishes to survive as a significant and long-term player in the industry.

From where can the business corporation derive its moral standard?

Three options are worth exploring: the self-interest of the corporation itself, a global ethic based on a rational humanistic foundation, or a revealed religion such as Judaism, Islam or Christianity.

The idea that the corporation can supply its own ethic is an intriguing one. Francis Fukuyama in his recent book *The Great Disruption* states that 'the assertion that a virtue like honesty necessary for commerce must depend on religion for its survival is, in the end, absurd. The self-interest of businessmen is sufficient to ensure that honesty (or at least the appearance of honesty) will continue to exist.'[5] He goes on to argue that 'the corporation that requires a high degree of honesty and civility in its customer service, or the firm that immediately takes a defective product off the store shelves, or the CEO who takes a pay cut to show solidarity with his workers during a recession are not acting altruistically: each has a long term interest in a reputation for honesty, reliability, quality and fairness or for simply being a great benefactor. These virtues become economic assets and as such are sought after by individuals and firms interested only in the bottom line.'[6] This

---

5   Francis Fukuyama, *The Great Disruption*, Profile Books, London 1999, p. 254.
6   ibid, p. 256.

argument recognises that honesty, like trust and cooperation, is a social virtue which builds up the social capital of an organisation. Fukuyama goes on to argue that social capital should not be thought of as a public good, the supply of which will be underprovided through the workings of a free market. Rather it is a good which private markets will provide in just the right measure as it is in the interests of corporate executives to supply it. Individual corporations typically build up their social capital by investing in education and training and management development programmes.

The intellectual foundation for this approach has been set down rigorously by Friedrich Hayek[7] and used especially by economists such as Milton Friedman and Gary Becker. Hayek argues that the market economy is but one, and a rather specific example, of what he terms a spontaneous order: namely a system which has developed not through the central direction or patronage of one or a few individuals but through the unintended consequences of the decisions of myriad individuals each pursuing their own interests through voluntary exchange, cooperation, and trial and error. This process of spontaneous evolution is not restricted to explaining the growth of the economic order but can also account for the development of language, money, culture, law, social conventions and even morals and ethics. Although the spontaneous order develops through individuals pursuing their own interest, the individuals still behave by following commonly held rules rather than by acting in a random fashion, and these rules are themselves the product of evolution.

---

7   The fullest treatment of this subject is in the three volumes of *Law, Legislation and Liberty*, Friedrich Hayek, Chicago University Press, Chicago, vol. I, 'Rules and Order', 1973, vol. II, 'The Mirage of Social Justice', 1978, vol. III, 'The Political Order of a Free People', 1981.

As a result ethics for Hayek are an important aspect of the social order: in fact the social order could not exist without 'rules . . . which lead individuals to behave in a manner which makes social life possible'.[8] But these rules are the result of a process of cultural evolution which emphasises the 'winnowing or sorting' of institutions and group practices. 'The cultural heritage into which man is born consists of a complex of practices or rules of conduct which have prevailed because they made a group of men successful but which were not adopted because it was known they would bring about the desired effects.'[9] At the same time Hayek is dismissive of any attempt to anchor ethics in religion, in a belief in God, or to suggest that ethics are immutable. The key to understanding Hayek's ethics is that they are the result of a long process of cultural evolution, which can be explained *wholly* within the self-existing natural order, in which individuals pursue their perceived self-interest. The moral order which emerges in Hayek's philosophy therefore is, in its entirety, a product of human endeavour and in order to avoid any possible misunderstanding he is explicit in his rejection of the need for something outside of the natural order in which to ground ethics. It is an ethical system as a result which is totally relative, without any firm absolutes or concepts of right and wrong. The irony of Hayek's approach is that although he rejects any religious foundation for the existing moral order, he nevertheless recognises the important part as a matter of history that religion has played in fashioning the rules to which he attaches such weight. In fact in his characteristically generous manner he goes out of his way to acknowledge his debt as an agnostic to believers.

---

8   ibid, vol. I, p. 44.

9   ibid, vol. I, p. 17.

The question which self-interest as the basis for a moral standard raises is how dependable and robust such a standard will be. Fukuyama argues that self-interest can be relied on to ensure that honesty, or at least, to quote him, 'the appearance of honesty', will continue to exist. But it is precisely in glossing over this distinction that he exposes the weakness of his argument. Many years earlier C. S. Lewis posed the question in the following way: 'Is there a difference between a man who thinks honesty is the best policy and an honest man?' He was convinced, as many have subsequently been, that the answer is yes.

The reason is that while the pursuit of self-interest may well result in a company wishing to secure a reputation for honesty, the pursuit of self-interest by itself will not result in a commitment to integrity or truth being enshrined as an absolute at the heart of the company which everyone in the company has a responsibility to acknowledge and by which they should be prepared to be judged. The reason is self-evident: there will be situations in which honesty is not in the best interests of the firm; and if the probability is very high that no one will be found out, dishonesty will pay so that the reputation of the company need not suffer.

The consequence of pursuing the appearance of honesty rather than honesty itself will be a lack of integrity at the heart of the corporation and the acceptance by management of double standards. The leadership and senior management of the corporation will be recognised for what they are, hypocrites. As dishonesty is condoned more and more, and double standards become the accepted practice, it is only a matter of time before some scandal becomes public. Without corporate leadership convinced of the existence of absolute standards which have a validity independent of their own self-interest and to which they must submit, it is difficult to see how a company could continue to include honesty among its core values. The crooked timber of humanity in which self-interest resides is too insecure a foundation on which to build lasting moral absolutes. Something more than the self-interest of business executives is needed.

An alternative basis for a moral standard in business is some form of global ethic based on shared human values and incorporating the views of the world's religions and ethical traditions. Such an alternative will recognise that religion remains a powerful force in the world but will also accept that for many people secularisation has meant an emancipation from religion. Even though secularisation will encourage individuals to conceive of themselves as autonomous and true heirs to the Enlightenment, there will remain still a strong drive for a basic moral orientation and a binding value system based on common human values, which could be widely accepted and recognised as a standard for behaviour. The objective of those who support this approach is to construct a global ethic which draws on the great religious traditions but which can at the same time be supported by non-religious people.

The person perhaps who is most identified with this project is the theologian Professor Hans Kung of the University of Tübingen, who has spent a great deal of time and energy seeking to develop a new global ethic as the foundation for a global society and who sees such an ethic as bringing together the necessary minimum of common human values, criteria and basic attitudes.[10] The Council

---

10 See in particular Hans Kung and Helmut Schmidt (eds.), *A Global Ethic and Global Responsibilities: Two Declarations*, SCM, London, 1993; Hans Kung (ed.), *Yes to a Global Ethic*, SCM, London, 1995; Hans Kung, *A Global Ethic for Global Politics and Economics*, SCM, London, 1997.

of the Parliament of the World's Religions which met in Chicago in 1993, incidentally the first such gathering of its kind in history, commissioned a Declaration towards a Global Ethic. This Declaration was based on the twin principles that every human being should be treated humanely and that you should do to others as you would wish yourself done by. It covered all aspects of life including business and involved key commitments to such things as a respect for life and a just economic order emphasising in particular the principles of solidarity, truthfulness, tolerance and equal rights. Although it did not develop a specific business ethic, its approach is very much in the tradition of the Code of Ethics presented at the Davos management forum in the 1970s[11] and the Principles for Business which emerged from the Caux Round Table (1980),[12] and it even has certain features in common with the Interfaith Declaration on a Code for Ethics for International Business from St George's House, Windsor,[13] though the last of these was confined to an inter-faith statement by Jews, Christians and Muslims. In terms of their approach to business, all three of these statements emphasise responsibility to stakeholders and not just shareholders, the basic values of human dignity, truth, fairness, mutual respect, service and a sense of moderation and modesty. The global ethic outlined by Kung emphasises, in addition, the need for a new social consensus which would be tantamount to a new social contract being drawn up between labour, investors and government.

The strength of the global ethic approach is that it accepts plu-

---

11   See Rosemarie Fiedler-Winter, *Die Moral Der Manager*, Seewald Verlag 1977.

12   *Caux Round Table Principles for Business*, 1980.

13   Interfaith Declaration. *Code of Ethics on International Business for Christians, Muslims and Jews*, Interfaith Foundation, October 1993.

ralism and secularism and rejects moralism and fundamentalism. It is inclusive, contemporary and carries no baggage from the past. It has been designed specifically for the modern global economy. The problem I have with it, however, has to do with motivation. To put it at its most simple, why should someone practise a global ethic? Although it is challenging, it is not in the end difficult to construct a comprehensive, humane and appropriate ethic for business which could be accepted by believers and non-believers alike. But the design of an ethic and the attempt to put it into practice are two entirely different things. The Declaration is honest enough to recognise that life on our planet, including the life of business, cannot be changed for the better 'unless the consciousness of individuals is changed'.[14] This is a demanding requirement. Hence the pledge which is made 'to work for such transformation in individual and collective consciousness, for the awakening of our spiritual powers through reflection, meditation, prayer or positive thinking, for a *conversion of the heart*. Together we can move mountains!'[15] (emphasis mine). The problem with a global ethic is that it will of necessity be the lowest common denominator of values between the religious and the non-religious. As such it cannot and will never be able to give an answer to those questions tackled by religion, such as the meaning of life; or to provide a set of unconditional values, norms and ideals as a standard of behaviour; or to hold out a sense of hope which is grounded in history; or to emulate the call for individual commitment made by an all-powerful but all-loving God whose service is perfect freedom. As the Declaration makes quite clear, living a global ethic

---

14   Hans Kung and Helmut Schmidt (eds.), *A Global Ethic and Global Responsibilities*: *Two Declarations*, SCM, London, 1993, p. 31.

15   ibid, p. 32.

requires a transformation of consciousness, a conversion of the heart, but without religion it is hard to imagine how such a conversion will take place.

The third option as a source for a moral standard is a revealed monotheistic religion such as Judaism, Islam or Christianity. One of the great strengths of these religions is that the standard has literally been written on tablets of stone and recorded in a Book. Although there are some complex issues involved in using the Commandments as the basis for a moral standard in a modern corporation, the Commandments not only embody an objective set of moral absolutes but also bring with them the obligation to obey the moral law. As a matter of history the Judaeo-Christian religion has been the bedrock on which many businesses have been developed, especially in Britain and America. Many companies which are household names have had as their origin a strong religious influence: Cadburys, Rowntrees, Barclays, Wedgwood, Unilever, Laing to name but a few. While a religious approach to ethics shares a number of insights with other philosophical but non-religious approaches, such as the recognition of an innate sense of moral obligation, an intuitive awareness of moral distinctions, a conception of a perfect world and the importance of striving towards a moral goal, the distinctiveness of the religious approach is that its ethics are grounded in religion. In the Old Testament the world and we who inhabit it are part of the created order and the motivation for an ethical life is obedience to the revealed law and ordinances of God, by a people, the Jews, with whom he has entered into a covenant. A statement such as Psalm 112, 'Blessed is the man who fears the Lord, who finds great delight in his commands', could be found many times over in the Old Testament. In the New Testament the basis on which the individual is invited to respond to the ethical demands of the gospel is the life, death and resurrection of Jesus Christ. Hence the statement of St Paul to the church at Ephesus, 'I urge you to live a life worthy of the calling you have received' (Ephesians 4), is repeated in similar form many times over in the New Testament.

Although there are crucial differences between the three monotheistic faiths mentioned earlier, they do have a common basis of moral and religious teaching and they all ground their ethics in religion. The Code of Ethics for International Business which was the result of a consultation on this subject picked out four aspects of this teaching as it was relevant to business. One was the principle of justice or fairness; another was mutual respect or reciprocal regard, 'love thy neighbour as thyself'; yet another was stewardship or trusteeship as a delegated responsibility to mankind for God's creation; and finally there was the principle of honesty or integrity, which incorporates truthfulness and reliability.

The strength of the religious approach embodied in a legal code such as the Ten Commandments is that each individual commandment is absolute, with the clear injunctions 'thou shalt' and 'thou shalt not'. Its rules are specific and provide a sanction on people's behaviour. It has stood the test of time. Despite the many changes over the centuries in the development of language, culture and economic structures the revealed religions have shown an extraordinary ability to adapt to new circumstances without changing their core beliefs.

The weakness of the religious approach is that in a modern or postmodern world it embodies an essentially premodern world view. While it is true that the moral capital of the Judaeo-Christian heritage has been diminished through secularisation, especially in

Europe, a case can still be made that religion remains powerful and has in fact been strengthened throughout recent decades by a series of significant publications and statements by churches and religious leaders. For example, since the early 1960s there have been no less than fourteen papal encyclicals dealing with business and economic issues. The statements by the Catholic bishops in the US in the 1980s on the US economy, and by their counterparts in this country in the 1990s on the relevance of the notion of the common good to economic life, have been influential documents. In Britain there has been a lively debate on the justice of a social market economy and the corresponding responsibilities of the business community following the publication of a report entitled 'Faith in the City'[16] in the mid-eighties, which was set up by the then Archbishop of Canterbury Lord Runcie. Professor Robert Fogel, a Nobel prize winner in economics at the University of Chicago, has argued in a fascinating new book, *The Fourth Great Awakening*, that since the late 1950s and early 1960s America has witnessed a religious awakening, the fourth in its history, which has set a new agenda for social and political reform which is both moral and spiritual. Although he does not develop it at length in his book it is hard to see how such a movement would not have an impact on business life.[17] Despite secularisation and the growth of postmodernism, therefore, religion remains a lively force in the US and, because of the influence of US corporations, on global business.

In grappling with the second question therefore, 'From where can the corporation find its moral standard?', there is clearly more

---

16 Archbishop of Canterbury's Commission on Urban Priority Areas, *Faith in the City*, Church House Publishing, London, 1985.

17 Robert William Fogel, *The Fourth Great Awakening*, University of Chicago Press, Chicago, 2000.

than one answer. For a moral standard to be meaningful it must be concrete and practical and not vague and an abstraction: it must be robust, it must stand the test of time; it must be seen as equitable and embody wisdom. It must be capable of exercising a radical impact and providing an effective sanction on behaviour.

Judged by these criteria, I am very doubtful whether self-interest as the source of a moral standard is sufficiently robust or whether it has the strength to influence behaviour. There will always exist the temptation to trim, to conceal and to mislead. A humanistic global ethic is open to question because of its explicit recognition of the need to transform consciousness but without the means to do so. From this point of view religion is powerful. A religion such as those mentioned which sees business as a vocation or calling, so that a career in business is perceived as a life of service before God, is a most powerful source from which to establish, derive and support absolute moral standards in business life.

How does a moral standard function and how can it be implemented in a pluralistic society?

For a moral standard to function in a corporation it is vital that it is set out explicitly. As a result, on joining the corporation everyone will know exactly what kind of organisation they are joining and precisely what is expected of them. Such a standard can be set out in the mission statement or the objectives of the corporation, in its business principles, through training programmes and speeches, in the annual report, and through activities which the firm may choose to sponsor.

It is important when implementing a moral standard in the pluralistic society in which we live that the standard is accepted by those who work for and invest in the company. Even though the corporation is not a democracy, standards cannot be established without the tacit consent of those who work for the corporation. People must own the standard for themselves. If they do not, the standard will be worthless, or worse still, a number of different standards may emerge, which is a certain recipe to create confusion. If employees reject the standard they can walk away and seek employment in another company whose standard they prefer. Similarly, if the shareholders do not buy into the standard, they can sell their stock but, possibly worse, they can also hold on to their stock and campaign against the values of the company by creating trouble at shareholder meetings. To make matters worse they could be supported by customers protesting in a very public fashion, prepared to take their business elsewhere, and by communities in which the corporation has facilities protesting through the political process. If people are to own the standards which the corporation sets out, the standards themselves must be seen to have a practical purpose: to provide better service to customers, to improve the quality of sourcing, to treat employees with dignity, to give help to employees facing change, to offer opportunity and to improve the quality of life within the company.

The leadership of a company has a specific and important role to play in maintaining its stated moral standard. The example set by leadership will speak powerfully about the importance the corporation attaches to its values so that, above everything else, leaders must themselves personally live by the standard. Setting out the standard in a reasoned way and making clear the principles on which it is based and the ramifications it will have in all areas of corporate life are important. But that is only a part of the story.

Aristotle in his *Ethics*[18] made the important distinction between intellectual virtue and ethical virtue. 'Ethical virtue is for the most part the product of habit (ethos) and has indeed derived its name, with a slight variation of form, from that word. . . . Our moral dispositions are formed as a result of the corresponding activities . . . It is therefore of no small moment whether we are trained from childhood in one set of habits or another: on the contrary it is of very great or rather supreme importance.' This insight, namely that the formation of a habit is of supreme importance in developing ethical behaviour, is typically associated with the raising of children, but it is just as relevant for the implementation of a moral standard within a company.

This suggests that the habits which characterise the way a company goes about its ordinary everyday business are important, because it is these habits which people will identify as the real values of the corporation: the respect given by management to individual employees, the care they take over their career development, the openness of divisional leaders in presenting their budgets and results, the choice of candidates who are put forward for promotion, the way in which breaches of the company's moral standard are handled, the treatment of underperforming executives, the openness of leadership to contrary advice, and so on. If people observe that the corporation adheres to its chosen standard in a consistent way, then the practices which they observe on a daily basis become a habit and have the power to strengthen the company's standard; if on the other hand there is a lack of consistency, with difficult issues not being faced up to and individuals exempted from the

18   For a useful discussion of Aristotle's *Ethics* see Alisdair MacIntyre, *A Short History of Ethics*, Routledge and Kegan Paul, London, 1967.

standard because of their star quality, this too will be quickly observed, and new habits will be formed which in time will detract from the standards which the company has set itself.

In implementing the standard the leadership of the company is never one person, the CEO. If a standard is to be established successfully there must be a core of committed leaders at the highest level who are prepared to champion it, and at the same time leadership throughout all levels of the organisation must be prepared to make it a priority. This has one major implication for recruitment and staffing. One criterion in recruitment policy should be that people hired should accept the explicit values of the corporation: those who cannot and will not should be rejected. One, but let me emphasise only one, consideration in moving people throughout the organisation is to ensure that those who embody the company's culture are placed in positions from which they can exercise a major influence on the organisation. On the other hand, nothing is more debilitating to team spirit if promotion is based primarily on conformity to cultural norms but without the individuals concerned possessing the skills to carry out their new responsibilities.

While it is impossible to prove conclusively, I believe that over time an independent moral standard is not only something which is good in itself but is also in the interests of shareholders and employees. Such a standard is never a substitute for other levels of management, such as strategy, systems, infrastructures or talented executives. But over time honesty will be seen to build up trust, people will respond differently when treated with dignity, a better quality of service will build up customer loyalty, and there will be reduced turnover of customers and staff. A company which adheres to a standard will find it is put to the test every working day and every working day will make a difference one way or another.

How significant is the corporation in our society because of its adherence to a moral standard?

Although it is rarely given sufficient credit, the modern business corporation has become an important standard bearer of values in our society. The reason it does not receive due credit is because in the minds of many people the corporation is identified with the maximising of profit or shareholder value, which is perceived to result in monopoly, cartels and high prices, fat cat compensation for executives, financial scandals and the taking of risks with the environment, all of which are rightly condemned as being against the public interest. This is a complex subject which cannot be dealt with at length here, but the following points are significant.

First, most modern corporations have an explicit set of standards which embody strong moral judgements, are in the public domain and are demanding in terms of the behavioural standards they set for all who work for the corporation. Second, with the decline of the church and the breakdown in family life in the West, the corporation has become an increasingly important community in its own right in which people spend a great deal of their time, and typically an important group from which they form significant friendships. Third, the corporation is increasingly a vehicle through which people contribute to charitable causes, both in cash and through programmes such as mentoring. Fourth, partly because of the track record and reputation of the private sector for the efficiency with which it manages its resources, but also partly because of corporations' explicit adherence to values, private sector corporations have been called on to run public institutions such as underperforming schools and to play a more significant role in the provision of welfare and health care services, something which would have been inconceivable a few decades ago. Fifth, individuals are able to achieve their own personal development through the training programmes and responsibility with which they are provided within the corporation. Sixth, in the area of training the public sector is looking more and more to work in partnership with the private sector in order to implement programmes of training and lifelong learning. And seventh, increasing emphasis on good corporate governance in many Western countries, linked to regulatory requirements which require greater transparency on the part of corporations, gives them an important global role in raising standards of accountability in countries still struggling to raise standards.

Conclusion

The concept of the corporation as a moral community is only one facet of business life. It is rarely high on the agenda because its impact is difficult to measure and its influence long term. But, managed well, the explicit establishment of a moral standard within a company can bring significant benefits to everyone associated with the company.

2 THE CULTURE OF VIRTUE, THE CULTURE OF THE MARKET
Robert A. Sirico

Introduction

I have chosen 'The Culture of Virtue, the Culture of the Market' as the topic of my remarks today because the relationship between the two is truly at the heart of the Acton Institute's mission. The culture of the market and the culture of virtue are often posed as competing sets of values, and at times with good reason. Many who proclaim the culture of virtue fault the free market for devaluing human life and turning the human person into a '*Homo economicus*', valued only for his earning potential or productive capacity.

I find this critique, advanced widely in the academy and among the clergy, to be myopic, even though it is born of a real and legitimate concern for the dignity of human life and the enhancement of a culture that protects the human person in all his complexity. It is myopic to the extent that it fails to make some important and crucial distinctions I will discuss in due course, and thus relinquishes what could be a powerful tool in the construction of a civilisation centred on the immortal destiny and the unique potential of every single person.

It is true that our times are characterised by a lack of respect for the dignity of the human person. But it is a great tragedy to see those who would be our allies against some of the forces that degrade the human person become hindered in their efforts as a result of a serious misunderstanding of the market economy. I believe that the dynamism of the free economy can be harnessed in support of the culture of virtue. The interaction and tension and ultimate reconciliation of the culture of the market and the culture of virtue are subjects worthy of deeper reflection.

The culture of virtue

But first let us be clear about the definitions. The culture of virtue is the recognition that this human life on earth is not the ultimate but rather the penultimate reality (*Evangelium Vitae*, ch. 2),[1] and that our earthly existence implies an end beyond itself, a telos of our eternal destiny. This life is a temporal stage, a passing ground, to our eternal existence, so that contained within each of us is the seed of eternity. C. S. Lewis put it poetically when he said:

> There are no ordinary people. You have never talked to a mere mortal. Nations, cultures, arts, civilisations – these are mortal, and their life is to ours as the life of a gnat. But it is immortals whom we joke with, work with, marry, snub, and exploit – immortal horrors or everlasting *splendours* . . . Next to the Blessed Sacrament itself, your *neighbour* is the holiest object presented to your senses.[2]

Life is a gift entrusted to us by our Maker. And it is to be preserved with the utmost responsibility and care. Since life itself is a gift from the Creator, it carries a sacred value from its inception to its end, and every human being has the right to have this life respected to the fullest extent possible. Therefore, any ethic which

---

1   Pope John Paul II, *Evangelium Vitae*, 25 March 1995, no.39.
2   C. S. Lewis, *The Weight of Glory and Other Addresses*, Collier Books/Macmillan Publishing Co., 1980, p. 19.

does not reflect the dignity of the human person must be opposed because it threatens the foundation of civilisation, it fights against nature and destroys the very context in which any rights can be enjoyed by anyone.

Any ethic which, for example, allows for murder, genocide, including chromosonal genocide, and the ghastly antics of the likes of a Dr Kevorkian in the US, is contrary to the culture of virtue. Any ethic which sanctions violations against the dignity of the human person, such as slavery, unjust imprisonment and prostitution, is contrary as well. And so is any system which treats people as mere instruments to greater gain, rather than free persons with inherent dignity (*Evangelium Vitae*, ch. 2).

The culture of virtue strives to protect the human person, including the most weak and defenceless. It is a culture of inclusion, charity, and peace. It answers affirmatively the Biblical question 'Am I my brother's keeper?'

While this ethic is concerned first for the spiritual aspect of the human person, it is also committed to his quality of life. It must strive to alleviate human suffering, and be concerned for the widest possible distribution of the earth's resources.

The culture of virtue and the social order

The human dignity of life can only be protected by a moral social order, those rules of conduct that keep society from chaos. The social order, as Russell Kirk has told us,[3] is bigger than its laws, though laws are born of it. The social order also includes the customs, manners, and beliefs of a society. To understand it properly

---

3   Russell Kirk, *The Conservative Mind*, Regnery Publishing, Inc., Washington, 1995, p. 68.

we must also recognise that the larger civil social order is intertwined inextricably with the character of the individuals who make up the society. If there is a moral decline, meaning a marked disorderliness in the individual souls that comprise society, the civil order will suffer.

While we may ardently desire human dignity to be reflected in our positive laws, that is not sufficient. I sometimes fear that, with our justified effort to ensure that laws are passed which promote a culture that supports and augments the dignity of the human person, our attention is deflected from the more fundamental obligation to ensure that our culture (including its social norms and intermediary institutions), which will be the context in which our laws are formulated in the first place, itself supports the dignity of human life.

The market promotes peace among men

Do people who value virtue have the freedom to choose among all available forms of economic systems to reinforce their values? I do not believe so. For example, consider how socialism views the human person. Under it, all individuals and all property are owned by the state, and all economic life falls under collective control. This has frightening consequences. For example, under socialism children are seen by the government as they are in fact: a drain on social resources. As Ludwig von Mises wrote, 'without coercive regulation of the growth of population, a socialist community is inconceivable . . . even if a socialist community may bring "free love", it can in no way bring free birth.'[4]

---

4   Ludwig von Mises, *Socialism*, Liberty Classics, Indianapolis, 1989, p. 175.

And he is right: every socialist experiment has led to forced abortion, euthanasia and limits on family size. For me, one great advantage of free enterprise rests in its dynamic ability to accommodate huge increases in the size of population without running the risk of famine. Only a liberal economy, and the growth of wealth it implies, has made this possible. Socialism makes it inconceivable.

Our own economic times are characterised by rising incomes, growing consumer and producer confidence, growing entrepreneurial opportunity, and exciting technological progress. Though political parties battle among themselves over who should receive the credit for these economic boom times, the credit actually lies elsewhere. The source of wealth creation now and always is the market economy.

The market is not a mere abstraction or system of economic production and distribution. The market is also people, those who actually do the saving and investing, take risks, keep contracts, watch the markets and live out their dreams. In their economic lives as producers, workers and consumers they are cooperating in a vast international network of market exchange, in which people half a world away they have never met buy their products and make products for their use.

For ages, philosophers sought an answer to the fundamental question of social theory: how is it possible in a social setting to achieve peace among people despite their differences? The success of the market economy provides one answer: they exchange. From the simplest to the most complex exchanges in the market, they all have one thing in common: people who trade voluntarily with each other – the very essence of the market – are doing so to their mutual self-satisfaction.

This has been called the 'magic of the marketplace' for good reason. We find it impossible to imagine that billions and trillions of dollars of exchanges can go on all around, and be the very source of our family's prosperity, yet we have the luxury of paying very little attention to the actual workings of this system. It is no wonder that the world has at last taken notice of the wonder that comprises this system of worldwide economic cooperation.

It is simply empirically inaccurate to suppose that the poorer nations of the world are getting poorer while the richer are getting richer. The fact is that, with the exception of those still experimenting with planned economies like Cuba and North Korea, the poorer nations are getting richer (for example Argentina and China) while some of the richer, owing to the expansion of centralised planning, are having a tough go of it (for example, Germany and France). In a recent paper published by the World Bank, David Dollar and Aart Krasy demonstrate that economic growth raises the income of the poor in the same proportion as everyone else.[5]

But the market does not work automatically; markets have no moral compass built in; the culture of the market also needs a moral precondition in the recognition of certain fundamental values. He who values the market must also value the sanctity of the human person, the broadest possible distribution of wealth, the greatest possible opportunities for economic creativity and a place for every person in the productive capacity of society. To be sure, that means placing strong emphasis on the indispensable institutions of private property, the freedom of contract, rivalrous com-

---

5   David Dollar and Aart Kraay, 'Growth Is Good for the Poor', World Bank, March 2000 <http.www.worldbank.org/research>.

petition and entrepreneurial enterprise; it also means understanding that these are not ends in themselves but instruments to be used to the higher glory of the Creator, the pursuit of virtue and of the common good, that is, the application of wide and generous opportunities for social mobility within the framework of security, freedom and civic virtue.

The market is the most powerful institution imaginable for making prosperity and productivity possible, for calculating and coordinating resources in society, and of course, these preconditions are as essential for assisting the poor as productivity is an essential precondition for distribution. Yet this productivity must be embedded in a social framework that is about something far more than mere profit and loss. The free society requires foundations that are moral at their very base: service, charity, duty, future-orientation and sacrifice. Contrary to the media stereotypes, the successful entrepreneur understands this all too well. Success in a market stems from the desire to serve others, both consumers and stockholders; the reward of monetary profit can be a driving force for motivation but it cannot be the basis of financial success itself. Competitive market forces demand that entrepreneurs always be outward-looking and service-oriented or they will lose their market share.

This outward orientation tends to shape the social perspective of the most successful entrepreneurs; it is not an accident that America's massive charitable sector is made possible by the wealthiest people in society giving of their resources. Charitable contributions also tend to grow in economic good times. To give to charity is a way of affirming that selfishness is not enough, and that ultimately we are all responsible for responding to a transcendent obligation to answer to a wide range of human needs, not just those we encounter in the marketplace.

It is crucial to remember that every person who participates in the market does so without coercion, but as an act of free will. To the extent that our actions serve the good of others, we benefit individually. And, conversely, if the market is cruel to anyone, it is to he who disregards the needs and values of his community and pursues a path of blind self-interest. Thus the market and the ethic of other-directedness are intertwined and mutually reinforcing, but not only for the owners of capital; the linkage extends throughout the entire network of work and exchange.

The culture of the market helps us fulfil God's command

The culture of virtue impels us to desire that all individuals with a vocation to work be allowed to do so. In Genesis, God calls the human family to what might be called an entrepreneurial vocation – 'be fertile and multiply, fill the world and subdue it' – a clear command to work and create. It is the market that offers people the best opportunities to employ their creative gifts and become full participants in society. The legal barriers and perverse incentives that have been erected by governments exclude people from the workplace, keeping many from perfecting their abilities and becoming a vital part of society's division of labour.

The culture of the market can also reinforce the culture of virtue in another essential way. The free market, the orderly and spontaneous cooperation among millions upon millions of individual actors, serves the material betterment of humanity. It has brought modern medicine, electricity, running water, and now information access to an ever broadening segment of the world population.

The culture of the market has often been characterised as a 'survival of the fittest' reality in which most individuals either produce enough as workers, or are harshly discarded by business and left to perish. Those of a collectivist mindset will have us believe that the market is actually a detriment to the poor. In truth, the politically unmanaged economy is the most efficient instrument for using resources and responding to human needs.

To illustrate, I would like to cite some examples offered by a man I considered a friend, the late Julian Simon, in his last article.[6] He wrote of attending a wedding and noticing all the attendees who ranged from well-heeled business executives to more casually dressed service workers. He thought of how even 200 years ago, nineteen out of twenty of those people's ancestors were living at or just above subsistence level. Since 1750 every indicator of the material well-being of the human population has vastly improved in most regions of the world. In England, for example, the average life expectancy was somewhere around the mid-thirties; by 1985, most English men and women were tending to live to about 70.

Simon points out that, much more than all of the tools and gadgets the market has brought to us, that prosperity represents the power to mobilise nature to our advantage. It allows us to extend and improve life through God-given technologies. The astounding intellectual breakthroughs in medicine are clearly at the service of the human person.

Because of the rise of market institutions, these material advances are not only for presently wealthy nations. In the coming decade, the average income in what we now call Third World countries will be about 80 per cent of the average per capita income of the United States in 1990, according to the calculations of

---

6   Julian Simon, 'Simon Said: Good News! There Are Fewer Constraints With Each New Generation', *Washington Post*, 22 February 1998, p. CO1.

economist Richard Easterlin.[7] And in our own society, those who live below the official poverty line enjoy a better diet than the European nobility of the eighteenth century. For 100,000 years mankind strove to consume enough calories, now the problem for masses of people is consuming fewer, as some of us know better than others.[8]

The flourishing of relatively free exchange has also created tremendous social mobility. The old leftist paradigm – in which every economic actor is either worker, owner or poor person – no longer gives an accurate picture of the economy. Whereas, twenty years ago, only the most wealthy invested in the stock market, now more than half of middle-income people invest. Ownership is being expanded to include more and more individuals. This means company profits have been democratised. And our hope should be for an ever-expanding economy to include more and more individuals.

Problems related to markets

But there are problems related to the market.

It is very unfortunate and highly dangerous that many of the market's most eloquent advocates often overlook the moral foundations of freedom. And to those who might be tempted to think society can revolve around the bank statement, we must be prepared to deliver a strong message: base motives can also exist within a market economy. The Congregationist minister Dr Edmund Opitz puts it this way: 'the market will exhibit every short-

---

7   Richard A. Easterlin, *Growth Triumphant: The Twenty-first Century in Historical Perspective*, The University of Michigan Press, Ann Arbor, MI, 1996.

8   Simon, op cit.

coming men exhibit in their thinking and peaceful acting, for – in the broadest sense – it is nothing else but that.'[9] Not all means of making money are automatically moral, and there are values higher than profit and market success. Among these values we must pre-eminently place the value of life itself.

As I have mentioned, new medical technologies are booming in many ways that advance the dignity of the person. We have medicines that can prolong a person's life; we have surgeries that can be used to aid babies *in utero*; we have drugs that can alleviate pain that would otherwise make an individual's life nearly intolerable. The market has made these advances possible, all to the enhancement of life.

Consider as a case in point: Professor Stephen Hawking. Thirty years ago he might have been left on the back ward of a state hospital, but through advanced technology he is able to make his insights and understandings (not all of which I agree with, I might add) known to a vast international audience.

However, with the advance of technology there are also new means of undermining life. The potential for human cloning is a case in point. The technology to be able to do something does not mean we ought to do it; as Acton says, 'The freedom of which we speak is not the freedom to do what we want, but the liberty to do what we ought', so that all our endeavours must be guided by that transcendental 'ought'. The purpose and justification of technology are that it serves the human community. But if human cloning goes forward it means that the human community may no longer beget our offspring, but *make* them, and what we make or create is

---

9   Edmund Opitz, *Religion and Capitalism: Allies, Not Enemies*, Foundation for Economic Education, Irvington-on-Hudson, NY, 1992, p. 80.

ours, thus debasing the dignity of human life and the concept of the inviolability of human rights and dignity.

The market must have a foundation in the ethic of life, or a godly ethic. And while ethical questions about life and death are certainly not always straightforward, given that there are limited resources in many life and death cases, these questions do not arise in a moral vacuum. Medical ethics and medical technology are different subjects, and the former must inform the latter.

Technological advance contains no inherent moral logic to guide it. If it is truly to serve the betterment of humanity, to serve the ethic of life, it must have objective moral norms to guide it.

Consumerism

What about consumerism, which is seen by many as the culture the market produces? It is a genuine and widespread problem that afflicts the soul. It arises when the end of our life is the accumulation of wealth and material pleasures. In this sense it is really a contemporary form of the ancient blasphemy of idolatry. But let us remember that when we talk about consumerism and materialism, we are speaking to problems of culture, not of economics. Indeed, while the market provides many temptations that we must resist, it also offers the means for overcoming them. It provides us concrete means to orient ourselves to an existence which looks beyond the here and now concerns. For example, the information revolution has brought us more opportunities for strengthening our faith: online. And it might be useful to remember that the act of reading the Bible is brought to us through entrepreneurship: once there was only a rather costly hand-copied version in the church and reading used to be something most people could not do beyond age 40 or 50, if they lived that long. Now electricity allows us to read into the darkness of night. Think of this: bedtime reading, an indulgence many of us engage in, would have been relatively unknown to most of our ancestors because of the lack of affordable books and electricity.

Advertising

Let me say a few words about advertising as a market function. It can be an educational tool, a legitimate means of competition, and a means to meeting needs. It is worthy of defence. However, there must also be a sense of responsibility in how it is used. For example, it should not encourage the consumer to see other people as mere objects. Sexual suggestiveness, which is often employed in advertising today, is a problem. It encourages the viewer, usually male, to look at the scantily clad woman as an object – all body, no soul, neglecting her human dignity – indeed denying the truth of who the woman is. This may be a new concept for the truth in advertising folks! And putting aside the facts of the various cases of tobacco litigation in the US, I think people are right to be wary of advertising campaigns crafted to market unhealthy products to the young.

A year or two ago, there was a massive outcry against the fashion industry, which had taken to using models that looked drugged out and strung out: the so-called 'heroin look'. This was an irresponsible use of advertising to draw people into paths that are destructive of life itself. To inform is one thing, but to corrupt is another.

Yet, it needs to be noted that the market is not simply about buying and selling. It is also about moral suasion, social outrage, boycotts and protests. All of these have a social function. It is perfectly legitimate and correct, for example, for traditionally religious people to encourage boycotts of sponsors that depict religion unfairly. Indeed, it is a responsible – and much needed – use of their voices in a free society. And the protests against advertisers who use corrupting techniques led the fashion industry to undergo a dramatic shift in its approach, suddenly giving way to what they called 'the happy look'. Through sheer social pressure, the industry has, for the most part, abandoned these tawdry techniques and embraced a more life-affirming approach to marketing.

Among the critics of the heroin look was the American president, Bill Clinton, who, interestingly, made some very powerful and appropriate remarks on the subject at the time. What was the philosophical basis of his comments? It stems from Communitarianism, an intellectual movement which came into its own during the Clinton era. This movement, which encompasses neoliberals and neoconservatives, argues that there is too much discussion today about rights and not enough about responsibilities. We hear about 'what society owes me' and not enough about our duties towards society.

This movement has provided a good corrective to a country that has come to reflect a strange combination of statism and individualism. However, we must look carefully at the Communitarians' solutions. If their moral vision for society calls us to have a greater respect for the common good, and makes fewer demands on what government can do for us personally, it is a good movement. But if it is merely being used as a cover for the further invasion of government power into the lives of our businesses, communities and families, then it is dangerous. It is worth noting that, after all, most of the problems the Communitarians identify are a result of too much government management of society, because government tends to divide people, not unify them.

Conclusion

Despite the failure of socialism as an economic system, it is still common to hear capitalism and the market economy disparaged for their failure to serve the interests of the human community. There is some merit in the charges. The profit and loss system is not the sum total of human community, and some defenders of the market think it is. A culture cannot ultimately be prosperous for any extended period of time without a cultural sense of values that are higher than material prosperity. There are values like fidelity, honesty and charity that must be drawn from moral foundations in the first instance if the material prosperity is to make sense.

What is generally underappreciated – because it requires serious thought to understand the causal connection – is the direct link between the accomplishments of the business sector, the advancement of social prosperity and the dramatic steps forward in health and human welfare.

The culture of the market can reinforce the culture of virtue. This message is one that needs to be brought to public debate. Radical libertarians who deny this are doing no service to the cause of economic liberty.

At the same time, we must help our allies in promoting a culture of virtue to understand that we are not for a go-go capitalism, which places the human person at the mercy of blind economic forces and which is not rooted in the fundamental ethic of life, person and property. What we propose is a free economy that puts the human person at the very centre of economic actions, simply because the human person is the source of all economic initiative. Let me energetically make the case that the market, imbued with freedom and virtue, is a necessary ally for a social order which respects human dignity.

I close with a set of complementary quotations from Alexis de Tocqueville and from Lord Acton.

Tocqueville wrote: 'Despotism may govern without faith, but liberty cannot. Religion is much more necessary in . . . democratic republics than in others. How is it possible that society should escape destruction if the moral tie is not strengthened in proportion as the political tie is relaxed?'[10]

And Lord Acton declared: 'No country can be free without religion. It creates and strengthens the notion of duty. If men are not kept straight by duty, they must be by fear. The more they are kept by fear, the less they are free. The greater the strength of duty, the greater the liberty.'[11]

---

10 Alexis de Tocqueville, *Democracy in America.* trans. George Lawrence, ed. J.P. Mayer, Harper Perennial, New York, 1988, p. 294.

11 Lord Acton, *Essays in Religion, Politics and Morality: Selected Writings of Lord Acton*, ed. J. Rufus Fears, Liberty Classics, Indianapolis, 1988, p. 650.

3   ETHICS, CONVENTIONS AND CAPITALISM
Norman Barry

The attacks on capitalism continue with the demise of communism but this time they come from a different source, one which is superficially more favourable to the private property/exchange system. The attack is ethical and rests on the unproven assumption that capitalism is ethically deficient. It has no ethical autonomy or integrity and this deficiency must be corrected from *outside* the market system. Its freedom is superficial and will lead to a breakdown of society if it is allowed full range. A great economist and spokesman for the market system expressed this view very well. Wilhelm Röpke, one of the intellectual founders of German *Ordoliberalism,* said:

> The market, competition and the play of supply and demand do not create ethical reserves; they presuppose and consume them. These reserves must come from *outside* the market. . . . Self-discipline, a sense of justice, honesty, fairness, chivalry, moderation, respect for human dignity, firm ethical norms. All of these are things which people must possess before they go to market and compete with each other.[1]

The idea that the market is fundamentally amoral is consistent with certain views of general morality in the twentieth century. For

---

1   W. Röpke, *A Humane Economy*, Wolff, London, 1960, p. 125.

a large part subjectivism about ethics dominated the debate, and logical positivism persuaded the intelligentsia that moral values were optional and no one set had any intellectual priority over another: social science was consistent with almost any set of moral values. Why not be a socialist if you could not produce either an intellectual or moral case for capitalism, or a Christian theologian if you are deeply unhappy with self-interest? But I will show that the market system is morally self-sufficient and it develops its own codes of conduct. Such rules would not satisfy the convinced positivist's demanding criteria for proof and demonstration but they are consistent with what we know about human nature and the 'laws' of social behaviour. I shall show that business morality develops spontaneously through the development of those constraints on immediate gratification which the market system undoubtedly requires. The rules are also consistent with what I call a minimalist or generic conception of social ethics and individual duty. Given the ubiquity of self-interest it can be shown that these conventions produce the optimal supply of virtue, that is, just enough to maintain the market. Any other duties are *supererogatory*, desirable but not compelling (indeed they are best exemplified in the non-market contexts of family and close personal relationships).

It is no coincidence that this view of ethics developed in the eighteenth century, just as the theoretical foundations of the market system were being laid down. Of the writers under consideration the most sophisticated was David Hume. Ironically, Hume is the intellectual godfather of logical positivism because he showed conclusively that ethics could not be given a foundation within his not exceptional account of human reason. They must depend on, and derive from, the *emotions*. Yet, unlike A. J. Ayer,

Hume demonstrated that certain virtues (the obligatory nature of promises, the binding features of exchange and the minimal rules of procedural justice) were essential to social stability and to commerce. In an instructive example he shows how two farmers who do not necessarily like each other, and indeed may not even know each other well, may still cooperate for their mutual advantage.[2] The point is that in most business relationships the participants are likely to meet each other in future transactions and have therefore an interest in enforcing common rules. They can also punish defectors from such rules and by a process of evolution non-cooperators are bred out. Business is a game that is repeated. Unethical conduct consists in the breach of such coordination rules for short-run advantage. Sometimes in the business world transactors know that they will not meet again and have every incentive to breach a convention. This can happen in the environment in situations in which property rights are ill-defined: a potential polluter knows that he will not live in the area which he damages and can avoid the informal punishment of his fellow business agents. They might all know that such malefactions will lead to the enforcement of unnecessary rules which make everyone worse off but, given reliable knowledge of human nature, good behaviour is unlikely to be voluntarily forthcoming. But as Hume insisted, the point is not to change human nature, which is the strategy of business moralists, but to devise rules that direct self-interested behaviour into socially productive channels. Such rules are properly universal, meaning they are requisites for civilised conduct – irrespective of religion or

2   D. Hume, *A Treatise of Human Nature*, H. Aiken (ed.), Macmillan, New York, 1948, Book III, pp. 61–2.

communal affiliations. Voltaire put the matter beautifully in his description of the nascent London stock market. He wrote:

> Go into the London Stock Exchange – a more respectable place than many a court – and you will see the representatives of all nations gathered there for the service of mankind. There the Jew, the Mohammedan and the Christian deal with each other as if they were of the same religion, and give the name of infidel only to those who go bankrupt. There the Presbyterian trusts the Anabaptist and the Anglican accepts the Quaker's promise.[3]

Indeed, in the established religions there was the early discovery of capitalism and a recognition of its moral features. Unfortunately, these very same religions came under the influence of twentieth-century moralism and dismissed capitalism's mainsprings as too redolent of greed and self-gratification.

It is my contention that a more expansive view of ethics actually undermines the acceptable morality I have just adumbrated. That subjectivism of logical positivism is reasserted with rival and competitive claims to rightness and fractious groups attempt to impose their conception of the good on economic organisations, especially business corporations. Hence the assertion of the community as a constraint on human action and the invention of the stakeholder as a rival to proper property holding. If we are to fill out the conventions to which I have just alluded we would have to talk about contract, respect for property, the demands of honesty in dealing and all the rules and practices that make commerce possible. Justice is limited to the enforcement of these practices and to the provision of rules that guarantee open access, but not equal ac-

---

3   Quoted in D. Boaz, *Libertarianism: a Primer*, Free Press, New York, 1997, p. 38.

cess. It is the mistake of modern business ethics to think that the supererogatory duties have the same moral force as these minimal standards. They are even given deontological force, hence the Kantian demand that there are moral claims which hold independently of utility. Thus firms ought to be socially responsible even when, perhaps especially when, such action results in shareholder loss; or the capital market must be characterised by level playing fields so that everybody gets an equal chance. But the capital market deals in information, the possession of which is invariably asymmetric.

The elements of Anglo-American capitalism

There are competing forms of capitalism in the world and contemporary business ethics has critically scrutinised one particular type, that practised in the United States, in the United Kingdom and in the English-speaking world in general. Although all the various types of capitalism conform to the generic moral code mentioned above, there are enough differences in how conformity to it is achieved to enable us to make some comparative moral judgements. Indeed, though erstwhile socialists might be reluctant to make wholesale onslaughts on capitalism, their preference for the more communitarian regimes of Japan and Germany derives from certain enduring features of Marxism. The important moral consideration here is individualism (often called greed or egoism). Apparently, other economies leaven the unadulterated self-interest of the Anglo-American economies with types of altruism. Otherwise, it is said, we have an antisocial bias and personal want-satisfaction is elevated above the common good.

This is not just a moral argument that prefers the intrinsic value of community over the individual, it is also a prudential warning that the behavioural patterns of classical microeconomics will so drain the person of any loyalty to essential social structures that individualism itself becomes unviable. Adam Smith worried that the decline of the 'martial spirit' under an advanced division of labour would leave market society vulnerable to 'republics', with their more militant social motivations. Nobody will defend the market, except for money. French critics of Anglo-Americanism have not dissimilar fears in mind when they protest at the import of alien cultural practices to their country under globalisation. Sometimes the objections are infused with a somewhat unsophisticated economics which denies that an invisible hand could ever coordinate the actions of dispersed individuals efficiently. Yet the smallest understanding of the knowledge problem in modern economies tells us that a market of individuals, guided by prices, coordinates information much better than any politically motivated institution could. In the face of such convincing evidence the moralists have resorted to the ethical objections to individualism.

But there is something disingenuous about this for the individualism of Anglo-American capitalism is not *atomised* individualism, an abstraction that precludes collaborative activity and the willing surrender of any amount of personal autonomy no matter how small. The assumption of some communal duties is not excluded by a concept of individualism that depends on cooperation.[4] Indeed, there might be some gain in the reduction of

---

4   See F. A. Hayek, *Individualism and Economic Order*, Routledge and Kegan Paul, London, 1948.

transaction costs by action of this type. But this is some distance from, say, the interruption of free trade by politically significant groups on behalf of some fictitious community, or the surrender of individual responsibility implicit in those philosophies, which would make corporations collectively liable for criminal actions. It is an important feature of the ethics of Anglo-American capitalism that individual responsibility for action ought not be shielded by a collective institution, that persons should not shelter behind the corporate veil.

The major institutions of the system can be explained in terms of individual interaction. Thus the corporation, against which so much criticism is levelled, and on which the supererogatory duties are normally imposed, can be explained entirely in terms of individual motivations and agreements. Although today the corporate form is regulated by statute this was neither historically the case nor is it required by theory. Permanent form, collective responsibility for civil actions and, most important, limited liability, can all be explained as the consequences of individuals pooling their resources and forming a common organisational structure under the common law. This is precisely what originally happened in the UK and the US; the role of the public authority was simply to register what were originally private actions.[5] In no way is the corporate form a gift from the state which has to be earned via the fulfilment of social and moral duties, as the former US Secretary of Labor seems to think.[6]

But the corporate form produces problems of its own. First, to what extent does it represent a loss in individual freedom? In a

5   See R. Hessen, *In Defense of the Corporation*, Hoover Institution, Stanford, 1979.
6   Reich thinks that corporate 'privileges' should be removed if companies do not fulfil certain obligations. Reported in *Reason*, July 1996.

sense it does, for the relationships that it produces are not quite like market relationships: they are not multi-contractual relationships in which each contractor trades with others, but are bilateral, specific deals between the worker and the employer (or resource owner) which bind the former to the latter in a 'master–servant' type of relationship. Second, the corporation involves a special problem scarcely noticed by conventional business ethics, the principal–agent difficulty. How can normally self-interested agents be relied on to fulfil their side of the contract and not behave in an opportunistic manner at the cost of the shareholder? Well, the takeover is the ultimate disciplinary device. Adam Smith's hostility to the corporate form derives from his nascent appreciation of the problem but he certainly did not anticipate the solutions to it that were to develop. However, business ethics writers often point to the successful non-Anglo-American economies that make little use of the method. Apparently they survive largely though a developed form of trust. Of course, trust is a part of the generic code of capitalism. This may be a feature of Kantian ethics which requires us to treat our business partners or employers as rational, autonomous agents who participate in non-contractual arrangements in a communal enterprise. Employers do not lay off workers at the slightest downturn and the latter abjure strikes and cooperate in the workplace. On the other hand, trust might have few moral features at all; it is just a way of reducing the transactions costs in a largely anonymous society.

Still, even in the context of a minimalist business ethics, trust is often overrated. In the US, although the country is reasonably high generally on trust, this may not be true of business. The stockholders do not trust the managers – they think they are opportunists and rent seekers – and the managers do not trust the shareholders who are, they think, short-termists who will sell their stock to a raider with little thought of the firm or those employees who have committed themselves to it and are highly vulnerable in the event of a takeover. But America is still the most successful economy in the world. It is also the one which fulfils the highest moral standards.

The major feature of Anglo-American corporate capitalism is the commitment to shareholder value. The reason why people pool their resources and become owners is to make money and the purpose of a corporation is to increase long-term owner value. Charities are, properly speaking, not businesses although it would be quite legitimate for a *private* owner to forgo profit on behalf of a moral principle. Ms Anita Roddick at one stage wanted to take the Body Shop private to be free of shareholder pressure[7] and Ron Hubbard, the leading business ethicist in New Zealand, runs an apparently successful private breakfast cereals company.[8] But publicly quoted companies are different for they involve complex *fiduciary* moral and legal relationships. The nominal owners of such companies are dispersed and normally take no direct part in management yet it has always been the case in English common law that the employees of such companies owe a strict duty to the owners (stockholders). Despite all the depredations that capitalism has experienced over the past hundred years that duty still remains (and was recently endorsed in the Hampel Report).[9] Companies are not forbidden from devoting part of their income to charitable activity (in some countries there are tax advantages

---

7   See Norman Barry, *Business Ethics*, Macmillan, London, 1998, p. 87.

8   See Norman Barry, *Anglo-American Capitalism and the Ethics of Business*, New Zealand Business Roundtable, Wellington, 1999, p. 23.

9   Committee on Corporate Governance, 1997.

in so doing) but there are limits to this and it cannot dilute the ultimate purpose and responsibilities of the business.

Although the pursuit of shareholder value might seem an uncontroversial aspect of business enterprise it is perhaps the one that has caused most dissent. Although it maximises the interests of millions of ordinary people, whose life savings, pensions and insurance are invested in the stock market, the pursuit of shareholder value has been linked with greed, the destruction of the environment, the dissolution of communities as a consequence of the onset of globalisation and other alleged horrors of the 21st century. I do not see how this can be an ethical problem. Those unhappy with the policies of, say, multinational companies are at liberty to invest in the many so-called 'ethical' outlets and the only objection here is to the implicit suggestion by the promoters of such schemes that investment in companies other than those on the prescribed list is somehow unethical. Activists have captured the word ethical itself, as they have appropriated 'rights'.

The attack on the shareholder value thesis has proceeded in two important directions: the invalid extension of the notion of fiduciary duty and the equally erroneous theory that company policy should not be directed (ultimately) by owners but by employee groups or coalitions of community activists (stakeholders) who might have no property rights in it at all. Both these strategies are directed at the individualism and property rights system that underlie Anglo-American capitalism.

The idea that fiduciary duties should extend beyond share ownership is morally appealing but economically makes no sense. The employees of a public company cannot serve two masters and if economic rationality is to be achieved it can only be by those who shoulder all the risks of investment. In fact, shareholders get little protection from the law: workers are protected by a myriad of employment protection laws and a number of non-discrimination decisions and statutes but stockholders are vulnerable to any passing political and moral fad: they have only their investment. Just recently a statute has been passed which requires pension funds to take account of social responsibilities in their investment programmes. At the moment the statute is permissive but one wonders how long we will have to wait before some onerous duties are imposed on them. But any extension of the social responsibilities argument must undermine property rights – for a property right is not just ownership of an asset but the freedom to use it in certain ways. Of course, all uses are limited significantly by law and morality but the limits derive from the genuine duties that business has.

But this is not what the advocates of social responsibility have in mind: they want to turn the supererogatory duties into compelling ones. Thus companies are 'instructed' to work for the community, to forgo profit if that is required for some moral goal to be advanced, to enforce affirmative action in the workplace even if that competes with marginal productivity theory in wage determination and to pursue other desirable things that are properly the responsibility of government, if they are anybody's.

It should also be noted that positive moral action of this kind often involves a breach of the basic deontological rule of treating people fairly. If company largesse is to be distributed away from the shareholders, what rules should be devised for the new allocation which would not disadvantage (perhaps arbitrarily) some groups? In the struggle for scarce resources that undoubtedly would ensue if companies did have the recommended extended fiduciary duties, it is unlikely that a principle would emerge that could secure more or less unanimous approval. Henry Manne quotes an instructive example from the 1970s.[10] Coca Cola ran a private enterprise welfare scheme in one of its less salubrious plants in Florida for some of its employees who were immigrants from Third World countries (where conditions were certainly worse than the original, unreformed Coca Cola plant). But such virtuous action simply raised the company's costs and unemployment resulted. Could morality provide a clear answer to the question of which group should be supported, current workers or the future unemployed? In examples such as this the firm tends to support the action which is publicly visible. But, as Bastiat reminded us, political economy is about what is not seen. Those rendered unemployable by the promotion of virtue were not visible.

Many companies today feel compelled to take on these social duties; they are replete with compliance officers and regularly publish reports which proclaim their moral achievements. In fact, this is not morality but prudence on the part of the firm (or rent-seeking by managements) in the face of mounting social pressure. Companies are constantly pressurised by shareholder activists who buy a small amount of stock and attend annual general meetings, not to encourage management to maximise shareholder value but to press social duties on them. Shell was for a long time a particular victim of this propaganda but it eventually surrendered; it appointed ethical compliance officers and published *People, Planning and Profits* in 1999. At the shareholders' meeting which discussed Shell's splendid moral progress a lonely stockholder

10   H. Manne, *The Modern Corporation and Social Responsibility*, American Enterprise Institute, Washington DC, 1972, p. 29.

commented: 'All very well but how come the stock price fell twenty-five per cent in the last year? Get real.'[11]

In fact, the only companies able to perform the demanding duties laid on them by business ethics would be monopolies. As an industry becomes more competitive there is much less slack left for fulfilling social functions. Indeed, it is noticeable how the privatised water companies, who are monopolists, have become very interested in social responsibility of late. But in normal markets, if a public company allowed its social responsibilities to affect adversely returns to owners, it would lose its competitive edge, the share price would fall and it would become vulnerable to a takeover. It is hardly surprising that those most active in the social responsibility of business movement are also highly critical of corporate raiders. Business moralist critics are faced with an awkward dilemma: are they to encourage or at least be silent about monopolists because they have the deep pockets that make it possible for them to do good, or are they to demand the breakup of monopolies on efficiency grounds? In addition, the absence of monopoly must also contribute to the ethics of capitalism by ensuring free and open access to the market and by providing conditions which make each participant a proper moral agent.

The stakeholder temptation

Perhaps the most serious threat to the integrity of the Anglo-American capitalist system from business ethics is the rise of the stakeholder doctrine. This poses a direct threat to property rights. The typical firm is constructed out of a complex structure of

---

11   Reported in *The Times*, 21 April 1999.

property rights and, most importantly, contracts. Indeed, the firm is a nexus of contracts. At the heart of the system are the control rights exercised ultimately by the owners; the board of directors is responsible for seeing that owners' interests are maximised and management is in charge of the day-to-day running of the firm. A whole network of fiduciary duties flows from these contractual relationships. Indeed, it is not so much ownership that determines who has the right to do what in the firm but the contracts that are made. A shareholder owns a little bit of, say, British Telecom, but this does not give him the right to break into its offices or use its secret information. The contractual nature of the firm assures that there will be a hierarchy and people who will play precise roles within it. It is most unlikely that the contracts made would depart significantly from the maximisation of shareholder value strategy.

But the stakeholder analysis decrees that positions occupied in the business derive not from contracts but from some arbitrary opinion of their importance within it. As leading stakeholder theorists Evan and Freeman say, 'The very purpose of the firm is to serve as a vehicle for stakeholder interests', and the reason for 'paying returns to owners is not that they own the firm, but that their support is necessary for the survival and that they have a legitimate claim on the firm'.[12] Note, the owners' claim is not decisive but it must take its place alongside that of workers, suppliers, members of the community in which the firm is situated etc. By a strange twist of Kantian ethics, which puts a rarefied notion of duty above any material or utilitarian consideration, Evan and Freeman have undercut the contractual and property basis of

---

12   W. Evan and R. Freeman, 'A Stakeholder Theory of the Modern Corporation: Kantian Capitalism', in T. Beauchamp and N. Bowie (eds), *Ethical Theory and Business*, Prentice Hall, Englewood Cliffs, 1993, p. 82.

modern capitalism. Indeed, it is nothing less than an attempt to politicise the firm in the name of ethics. It is redolent of Ralph Nader's attempt to democratise the corporation in the 1960s and 1970s. Indeed, it is for a very good reason that business ethicists refer to the groups that compete with stockholders for control of the firm as 'constituencies'. They want to politicise the firm.

The stakeholder theory of the firm makes no sense in terms of coherent decision-making and transparent management. No rational decisions would be possible under stakeholderism and the boardroom would resemble a parliament even more fractious than the ones with which we are already too familiar. It would be a prey to pressure groups which would most likely have no financial interests at stake. No doubt something like that goes on in regular companies but at least there is an ultimate ordering mechanism encompassing property, prices and profit, which resolves inter-group conflicts. Under stakeholderism there would be no such mechanism. If everybody is responsible then nobody is; if we all own property then nobody can claim exclusive use of it. Imagine the deadlock that would occur in plant relocation and the innumerable groups that would have to be satisfied before a decision could be reached. Indeed, the incoherence of the stakeholder theory can be shown by an application of a famous demonstration in social science and democratic theory – the Arrow theorem.[13] If there are at least three possible decisions and three voters and the matter is voted on one by one, 'cycling' results: no determinate winner emerges but three different ones and the matter has to be settled by a 'dictator'. This can only be avoided in rare circumstances,

13   K. Arrow, *Social Choice and Individual Values*, Yale University Press, New Haven, 1951.

circumstances unlikely to be reproduced in a company. Evan and Freeman seem to be aware of the problem of competing and incommensurable group interests but their suggestion for resolving such issues – the appointment of a 'metaphysical director' – is laughable. Of course, in a regular company the matter is settled by property and contract and there is a grisly consistency in the stakeholder theorist's recommendation of the replacement of conventional company voting by one share, one vote with one person, one vote. But the firm is not a democratic organisation.

All this is not to say that the idea of a stakeholder is completely misguided. It would be prudent for owners to treat people as if they were not easily dispensable labour units but had some significant role in the company quite apart from any property interests they may, or may not, have in it. Indeed, contractual relationships are by no means exclusively understood in terms of property. But all this is a matter of prudence not ethics, good business practice not metaphysics. And although ownership and contract are decisive they should not swamp all other considerations, especially if we are talking about those conventions and moral practices that predominate in business.

Takeovers

What really distinguishes Anglo-American capitalism from its rivals is its preference of the takeover method of industrial reorganisation and its use as a device for ensuring good management.[14] It might be the case that other forms of capitalism, perhaps those concerned more with communal obligations than shareholder

---

14   See Barry, *Business Ethics*, ch. 6.

value or with market share rather than profit and loss, do well without it. As measured by transactions costs, the takeover method might look, superficially, an expensive way of ensuring good conduct and the elimination of rent-seeking and opportunism. But the method has to be carefully analysed.

There are two major areas of interest for business ethics in the takeover mechanism. As the venue for shareholder value it raises the moral question of individualism. Does the pursuit of self-interest here eliminate all other values that might have significance in the maintenance of a free society and does the disruption to people's lives that it sometimes causes undermine social stability, order and predictability? Are some people who are the likely victims of the process, especially holders of firm-specific human capital (those whose skills are only appropriate for one firm), treated merely as means to advance the ends of others, a breach of Kant's fundamental principles of ethics? A second, logically distinct though related question is that of human conduct in the takeover process itself. Certain actions have provoked great hostility; I refer here to golden parachutes, greenmail, 'two-tier takeovers' (and the treatment of small shareholders) and the accumulation of debt as the most controversial examples. Some of the problems of the takeover are economic and the critics have challenged its efficiency properties. Takeovers lead to short-termism and underinvestment: there is no invisible hand that guarantees a neat harmony between individual gratification, it is claimed. How is it that some highly successful economies, notably Japan and Germany, have until very recently abjured the takeover's relentless individualism?

In fact, the takeover method is simply an extension of the freedom that the market guarantees and while debate has centred on the current wave, dating from the 1980s, there have been periods in history, in the early twentieth century for example, when it was even more intense. It occurs largely because someone notices that a company is being undervalued by the market and this rival entrepreneur thinks he can manage the assets better, that is, ensure greater shareholder value. He offers a premium to the existing market price and takes the company over. He probably dismisses staff, reorganises the firm and spins off unwanted parts, often to pay off the debt that the deal incurred. In the 1980s some takeovers were clearly a response to earlier inefficient takeovers that were management-driven and had led to inefficient conglomerates. In the 1980s, predators such as T. Boone Pickens sensed this and restored the original fiduciary duties of managements. They had failed to return money to stockholders but had embarked on ambitious expansions. Even more controversial were the sharks who broke up perfectly viable companies.

It is difficult to see anything wrong economically or morally with this. Indeed, a large part of America's current economic success can be traced to the massive industrial reorganisation that took place in the 1980s and 1990s. People like Michael Milken,[15] who struck fear into established corporate managements with the junk bond method of corporate finance, were acting on behalf of the long-neglected stockholder. The 'victims' of all this were not the workers, whose employment prospects expanded rapidly, but rent-seeking managements who slowed the process up in America by spearheading a campaign against the new methods; they were active in ensuring that most of the American states passed anti-takeover statutes in the late 1980s. Those countries that spurned the technique suffered accordingly. But it is spreading; in Italy

---

15   Barry, *Business Ethics*, pp. 141–4.

Olivetti pulled off a spectacular reverse takeover of the privatised telecomunications company. Even the powerful Agnelli family could not resist the lure of shareholder value. And in Germany the most expensive takeover in history, Vodafone's capture of Mannesmann, was achieved against tremendous stakeholder pressure. What was significant here was that it occurred after a group of shareholders threatened legal action to compel the management to fulfil its fiduciary duties. Even Japan has had a similar experience. The British company Cable and Wireless took over its privatised telecommunications industry against strenuous local opposition which included a rival Japanese bid. In Japan, shareholders are treated very badly by incumbent and irremovable managements. They are kept out of any control of the company, often by criminal acts, and are paid derisory dividends. Of course, shareholders' reliance on capital gains came to an end in 1990 with the collapse of the Tokyo stock market.

It is true that a lot of money is made out of takeovers, especially by financial and legal intermediaries. And shareholders do not gain equally. It is the stockholders of the target company who are the main beneficiaries; they have to be persuaded financially to part with their shares. And some of these rewards offend the prevailing egalitarian sentiment. But there need be no breach of justice. Anglo-American markets are remarkably open and fluid. Any immorality comes from incumbent managements who construct amazingly complex defence mechanisms against the raider, all of which deprive the stockholder of what is rightfully his. Again, two-tier takeovers (forbidden by the British Takeover Code) in which a higher price is offered to the stockholders who are required to sell in order for control to be achieved are not reprehensible. Shares command different prices at different times and it is a matter of first come, first served.

The most bitterly fought tactic is the poison pill, forbidden by the remarkably effective British Takeover Code. In this the articles of association, or charter, of a company are altered so as to make a takeover very costly. It is often used by management to benefit a suitor which it favours. This happened with the Warner capture of Time when Paramount had made a better offer. The pill here was upheld by the Delaware courts and this led to a slowdown in American takeovers.

Golden parachutes look unnecessary and seem to illustrate corporate greed on the grand scale. But they have a rationale. A raider might find it in his interests to buy off incumbent employees of the target company; they are often in a position to make the transition to new ownership difficult. Of course, it could occasionally be in the interests of opportunistic management to provoke a takeover in order to secure golden parachutes. But here what is required, as in so many other aspects of corporate government, is vigilant shareholders. To rely on external business ethics, which is often followed by coercive law, would be to undermine the company and the property rights it embraces.

The same applies to greenmail. This is where a potential raider is bought off with a higher price for his stock than is available to other owners. Despite the connotations of blackmail and ruthless self-interest, the ethical critics have the wrong target in mind. The guilty party is not the greenmailer, who is merely putting out a signal about the company, but the managements who often load a company with debt to ward off an unwelcome advance. They should simply refuse to pay and wait to see what happens. As in all these cases, business has every interest in developing appropriate rules and competition is the best guarantee of fairness.

Conclusion

Conventional business ethics overlooks the capacity for self-regulation on the part of business. Good ethical conduct does not require a change in the moral personality, it simply requires the capacity in business agents to follow those conventions which are to their long-run advantage. It requires that they be prepared to forgo opportunities to make immediate gains in the interests of sustaining these rules and conventions that make for long-run success. Normally, instant and objectionable profits arise in cases like the environment where property rights are not well defined. It may be difficult to persuade a person to act morally if he is never likely to see the victims of his short-sighted action, or take part in repeat games, but in such circumstances it is wise for the business community itself to devise those rules which automatically channel the natural desire for self-improvement in socially optimal directions. As David Hume said: 'as it is impossible to change or correct anything material in our nature, the utmost we can do is to change our circumstances and situation, and render the observance of the laws of justice our nearest interest and their violation the most remote'.[16] The generic moral code, from which Humean conventions derive their ethical validation, is the only one capable of uniting the varieties of capitalism under a common set of moral principles. And that is the only business ethics that globalisation requires.

---

16   Hume, *A Treatise of Human Nature*, Book III, p .220.

4 MARKETS AND THE PROVISION OF A MINIMUM INCOME IN RETIREMENT
Frank Field

Five years is but a moment in the life of a country like ours. But within the last five years the Labour Party's view of the market has been transformed. From a position of hostile engagement, the party is anxious to display its newly acquired market-friendly credentials. I remain fully supportive of this most fundamental of changes. But I would like to use this paper to place a question mark against the idea that The Market Rules, OK. I do so because it is a misreading of our history to think that that has ever been the position of the market, even under the heyday of Victorian capitalism. But the question mark is there for a second reason. While a fully paid-up member of the market brigade, I believe there are some areas of provision where the market cannot achieve socially desirable goals. I wish to illustrate one such area by looking at the best ways to achieve a universal minimum pension provision in this country.

The Victorian ideal

Much revisionist effort has been expended over the past few decades in considering how purely laissez-faire Britain was during part of the last century. I leave it to others to summarise this debate. What I wish to do here is to stress two aspects of that debate about markets which are missing from today's discussions.

Markets in the heyday of Victorian capitalism were buttressed by a set of moral beliefs which attempted to enforce a strict code on those operating in the market. The market was also buttressed by a substantial and growing non-market sector. The moral code, of course, came in the form of Christianity. There is no point attempting to gauge the extent of belief in Victorian times. What we can observe, however, is the extent to which Christianity's precepts were conformed to in public and private life, and how the elementary values such as honesty in the drawing up of contracts, for example, were informally enforced. The breaking of one's word could and did lead to an expulsion from the club.

The virtual collapse of Christianity as a system of belief in this country has led governments to attempt to regulate the market in different ways. Parliament has recently put on to the statute book a new Financial Services Authority which will attempt to enforce basic rules of honest behaviour in a way Victorians managed to do voluntarily. And, irony upon irony, the one person who has most successfully challenged the dominance of the market has been the pro-marketeer Conservative thinker Brian Griffiths. He, more than anyone else in recent times, has helped shape a debate which emphasises the importance of markets being operated by moral individuals. There have, of course, been Christian Socialist critiques of the market. But no one has had the impact on debate, and for good effect, that Brian Griffiths has achieved.

The operation of the market in Victorian times was not only gated by a nation of professed Christians. The political community also emphasised the value and importance of a growing non-market sector. Not only was this a time when the modern structure of local government was established but Victorians, in various degrees of enthusiasm, welcomed the existence of friendly and mutual societies, as well as trade unions. In modern day parlance they saw these bodies as key parts of civil society, important in themselves, but important also as bulwarks against central government power and therefore an essential part of a strong democracy.

The political class also lent weight to these counterbalancing forces to market dominance. By the third quarter of the nineteenth century much of the political elite was obsessed by attempts to ensure that the rise to respectable society of the skilled working class was extended still further along the class base of this country. How to spread this success became a key concern in policies to tackle the Condition of the People question.

Three political groupings gave strength and force to the direction of these policies. The Tories had always possessed a paternalistic wing. Liberalism was fast beginning to outgrow the constraints of the Gladstonian approach to political activity. And, by the turn of the century, the advent of the Labour Party was there for all who wished to observe. Each of these three political forces defended the existence of, and sought ways of nurturing, the non-market sector of civil society.

Damaging ideas

During the twentieth century, by contrast, both the left and the right launched damaging attacks on the best functioning of the market. Labour's contribution on this front came largely from its insistence, until recently, on holding Clause IV of its constitution as a legitimate end of political activity. I leave aside how undesirable it would be to live in any society which took Clause IV, part IV (to give it its full billing) to its logical conclusion.

Little noticed, but much more damaging, were the practical

conclusions which were drawn from the Clause IV debate. It assumed that the economic problem had been solved. The crucial question was one of a fair distribution of what the economic system produced. And to give this debate a further twist, as if that was what was required, R. H. Tawney, the most influential of twentieth-century socialist writers in England, emphasised that the whole economic system be run on the basis of service, rather than reward.

The embrace by the right, for a significant period, of Keynesian ideas also directed attention away from the functioning of the economy, to questions of its fine tuning. For decades British politicians became obsessed with demand-side issues, when the discussion should have been directed to the supply side of the economy: how to shift resources from a declining industrial base into new areas of growth and opportunities. Naturally, enough reaction against the dominance of demand-side policies has occurred. And, as with most swings of the ideological pendulum, this one has probably gone too far.

Non-market rule OK?

One of the most fruitful ideas of the nineteenth century was whether it was possible to establish a national minimum below which no member of society would fall. This is an ideal which still awaits fulfilment.

One of the most important areas where there is much government activity is in yet another attempt to extend pension provision in this country. Here two approaches are apparent.

The first is the long-established one of adding to existing provision, knowing that it will fall short of establishing a universal minimum. An alternative approach, and one I attempted to persuade the government to adopt while I was a minister, is to design a scheme which holds out the possibility for the first time of gaining a national minimum income in retirement free of means-tested assistance.

The pension proposals

For the sake of simplification I will call the government's proposals 'Stakeholder Pensions', and I will title the ideas I put forward as minister the 'Universal Protected Pension'. You will remember that the government has a three-pronged approach to pension reform. A new State Second Pension will be established for those on very low earnings up to £9,000 a year. For those workers crossing this threshold, but earning below £18,500 a year, the government is encouraging the private sector to introduce Stakeholder Pensions. For those people who are retired and poor the government has implemented a Minimum Income Guarantee. To all intents and purposes this is a variant of the income support scheme which it replaced, albeit at a more generous level of income.

The Universal Protected Pension I put forward is the only workable scheme that guarantees to break the link between retirement and poverty. The Universal Protected Pension, which will be a single product, stands in contrast to the government's approach of a multiplicity of pension products all being sold under the title of stakeholder pensions.

There are three other crucial differences between Stakeholder and Universal Protected. In the first place, Universal Protected Pension offers a pension guarantee which will ensure that all fully paid-up contributors will have a pension well above the means-tested MIG level. The guarantee will be brought about by combining the current pay-as-you-go National Insurance pension scheme with a funded savings scheme.

Second, because the guarantee cannot for most people be bought in the private market (the Richard Bransons of this world would be able to afford the premiums for such a guarantee, but they are unlikely to want a Universal Protected Pension), the scheme envisages graduated contributions for this flat-rate guarantee. The graduated contributions will raise the funds to include those who are at work, but at any one time on very low earnings, or who are outside the labour market but whose role, such as caring, is one which society wishes to reward by full membership of the Universal Protected Pension scheme.

The third difference between the two proposed pension schemes is that the Universal Protected Pension will be compulsory for all those in the labour market as they reach a certain age – say 25. Compulsion will result in much lower charges than the one per cent cap being set for the government's stakeholder products. Reducing this charge will make a significant difference to the size of funds underpinning the pension guarantee. The government's insistence on one per cent is not a cap on contributions, but the ceiling on charges on the whole of the monies being accumulated via a stakeholder product, that is the capital as well as each annual contribution. A one per cent cap, while sounding harmless enough, will still lead to a loss of in excess of 20 per cent of the total sum saved over a working life in a stakeholder pension.

Each of the many focus groups that companies have staged on stakeholder pensions has found that the one thing contributors to the groups most wish is to gain a pension guarantee. These contributors simply did not understand what was being meant by the sums being bandied about on the likely pension to be gained from a stakeholder product. Now, thanks to the calculations the Government Actuary undertook for the Social Security Select Committee, and the detailed work the Financial Services Authority has produced on the stakeholder decision trees, it is possible to compare current pension provision on the one hand, and the pension outcomes under the two proposed pension schemes.

The current pension provision and the Universal Protected Pension provision after 40 years, revalued back into today's prices, produced the following levels of pensioner income. The state pension for a single person is £67.50 a week. The Minimum Income Guarantee introduced by the government ranges for younger pensioners from £78.45 a week to £86.05 a week for pensioners aged 80 and over. In contrast, the Universal Protected Pension would offer a pension of £142.70 a week.

There are two important differences between the Stakeholder and the Universal Protected proposals. The first is that only the Universal Protected proposal offers contributors the certainty of remaining free of poverty throughout their retirement. While some, and I emphasise the word some, of the contributors to the Stakeholder Pension will initially gain a pension above the means-tested MIG level, many of these potential pensioners will soon fall back to dependency on the MIG. Stakeholder pensions will be indexed to prices. The Government Actuary calculations for the Universal Protected Pension assume that it will be raised in line with earnings.

The second difference between the two proposed pension schemes stems from the compulsory nature of the Universal Protected Pension and its guarantee to deliver a pension above means-tested assistance level. Currently the government's Minimum Income Guarantee undermines much if not all of the attractiveness of taking out a Stakeholder Pension. Most people for whom Stakeholder Pensions are targeted will not be able to save enough during their working life to make themselves better off than simply relying on the MIG when they retire. It does not require great powers of prophecy to foresee the negative effect the MIG will have on savings through the government's stakeholder scheme. In contrast, the Universal Protected Pension sends out a very different message. Because of the nature of the guarantee, every contributor knows that should they save additional money, or if they invest any winnings or inheritance, the income from these activities will be paid in addition to their Universal Protected Pension. That guarantee cannot be offered under the government's proposals.

The difference between the two proposed pension schemes can be seen clearly by taking a contributor on £14,000 a year – the mid-point of the Stakeholder target group (see Table 1 on page 88). Taking the calculations set out by the FSA, such a person contributing over 40 years, and drawing a full National Insurance pension, would have a combined income of £160.01 a week in today's prices. This sum would then only be increased in line with prices.

In contrast the Universal Protected Pension offers a guarantee, when combined with a National Insurance pension, of £210.20 a week in today's prices. Because the Actuary assumed that the funded element of this pension would be linked to average earnings growth once in payment, after 10 years this rises to £233.11 and after 20 years to £259.70 a week.

One last point is that the Select Committee concluded after reviewing the Government Actuary's calculations on the contributions to the Universal Protected Pension that a 9.9 per cent additional employee contribution on top of existing National Insurance rates makes it doubtful that people would be willing to pay contributions at the necessary level. But the 9.9 per cent is a gross figure. The government has already announced that rebates will be paid to ensure that those earning over £9,000 a year do not settle down to membership of the Second State Pension. The current rebates to opt out of SERPs stand at 4.6 per cent. Such a rebate is likely to be offered to contributors moving from the Second State Pension to the Stakeholder Pension. Assuming, therefore, an equal rebate for a Universal Protected Pension, the weekly percentage contribution is reduced from 9.9 to 5.2 per cent.

Conclusion

Through the issue of compulsory saving for retirement and redistribution within that saving I have tried to show how the debate about markets can move on from a simple acceptance or rejection of markets. Most people nowadays accept and embrace the huge beneficial effects of a market economy. I am one of them. But in some crucial respects, largely because of the inequality in earnings that all market systems produce, a market cannot provide what the community requires. One such example is a decent minimum income in retirement.

I have here looked in detail at the two proposed pension schemes. My analysis shows that the best buy for the community is the compulsory proposals as opposed to the free market proposals. Under a free market system the poor cannot save enough to be clear of the poverty level of benefits that the community provides and, I would guess, considers an unsatisfactory income for an elderly person. The alternative I have put forward is to make the poor save what they can and in return top up their contributions to give an acceptable pension. Where such a reform must engage with the market is in the safeguarding of the assets built up under the scheme, and in persuading people to save on top of their Universal Protected Pension.

Table 1 **Difference between Stakeholder and Universal Protected Pensions**

	Stakeholder Pension	Universal Protected Pension[a]	Universal Protected Pension with SERPS rebate
Age at first contribution	25	25	25
Age at retirement	65	65	65
Annual earnings	£14,000	£14,000	£14,000
Additional monthly pension contribution	£64.66	£82.90	£42.59
+Exchequer contribution	£18.24	-	-
+SERPS rebate[b]	-	-	£40.31
Total monthly contribution[c]	£82.90	£82.90	£82.90
Value of new pension per week at point of retirement	£92.51	£142.70	£142.70
+ Basic state retirement pension	£67.50	£67.50	£67.50
Total weekly pension at point of retirement	£160.01	£210.20	£210.20
Weekly pension 10 years after retirement	£160.01	£233.11	£233.11
Weekly pension 20 years after retirement	£160.01	£259.70	£259.70

a The plans for the Universal Protected Pension do assume that the standard rebate for salary related occupational pensions will be invested in the scheme. However, for comparison with Stakeholder this costing is done with rebates.
b The rebate level is here assumed to be the standard rebate for salary related occupational pension: 4.6 per cent of relevant earnings over the National Insurance band.
c This is equivalent to a 9.9 per cent increase in Employee National Insurance, which is the gross contribution (i.e. excluding SERPS rebates) that the Government Actuary calculated was required for the Universal Protected Pension.
d All National Insurance data is for 2000/2001.

ABOUT THE IEA

The Institute is a research and educational charity (No. CC 235 351), limited by guarantee. Its mission is to improve understanding of the fundamental institutions of a free society with particular reference to the role of markets in solving economic and social problems.

The IEA achieves its mission by:

- a high quality publishing programme
- conferences, seminars, lectures and other events
- outreach to school and college students
- brokering media introductions and appearances

The IEA, which was established in 1955 by the late Sir Antony Fisher, is an educational charity, not a political organisation. It is independent of any political party or group and does not carry on activities intended to affect support for any political party or candidate in any election or referendum, or at any other time. It is financed by sales of publications, conference fees and voluntary donations.

In addition to its main series of publications the IEA also publishes a quarterly journal, *Economic Affairs*, and has two specialist programmes – Environment and Technology, and Education.

The IEA is aided in its work by a distinguished international Academic Advisory Council and an eminent panel of Honorary Fellows. Together with other academics, they review prospective IEA publications, their comments being passed on anonymously to authors. All IEA papers are therefore subject to the same rigorous independent refereeing process as used by leading academic journals.

IEA publications enjoy widespread classroom use and course adoptions in schools and universities. They are also sold throughout the world and often translated/reprinted.

Since 1974 the IEA has helped to create a world-wide network of 100 similar institutions in over 70 countries. They are all independent but share the IEA's mission.

Views expressed in the IEA's publications are those of the authors, not those of the Institute (which has no corporate view), its Managing Trustees, Academic Advisory Council members or senior staff.

Members of the Institute's Academic Advisory Council, Honorary Fellows, Trustees and Staff are listed on the following page.

The Institute gratefully acknowledges financial support for its publications programme and other work from a generous benefaction by the late Alec and Beryl Warren.

Other papers recently published by the IEA include:

WHO, What and Why?
Transnational Government, Legitimacy and the World Health Organization
Roger Scruton
Occasional Paper 113
ISBN 0 255 36487 3

The World Turned Rightside Up
A New Trading Agenda for the Age of Globalisation
John C. Hulsman
Occasional Paper 114
ISBN 0 255 36495 4

The Representation of Business in English Literature
Introduced and edited by Arthur Pollard
Readings 53
ISBN 0 255 36491 1

Anti-Liberalism 2000
The Rise of New Millennium Collectivism
David Henderson
Occasional Paper 115
ISBN 0 255 36497 0

To order copies of currently available IEA papers, or to enquire about availability, please contact:

Lavis Marketing
73 Lime Walk
Oxford OX3 7AD
Tel: 01865 767575
Fax: 01865 750079
Email: orders@lavismarketing.co.uk